Table of Contents

Preface

In an era defined by screens and digital connections, the concept of careers has evolved into a dynamic landscape that tsranscends boundaries. The Internet, with its vast reach and endless opportunities, has given rise to unconventional online careers that empower individuals to explore new horizons, connect with others in unique ways, and redefine the very notion of work.

This book is a journey into the heart of the digital age, where innovation and human connection intersect. It delves into a realm where individuals harness the power of technology to create meaningful connections, share stories, offer support, and reimagine traditional notions of employment. Here, you'll encounter virtual friends and companions, online confidants, digital storytellers, and many more who have ventured beyond conventional career paths to make a difference in the world.

Each chapter is a window into a different facet of the digital universe, introducing remarkable individuals who have embraced unconventional online careers to illuminate the boundless possibilities that the digital age offers. These careers are not just about making a living; they are about making a difference, one virtual connection at a time.

As you embark on this journey, remember that the digital age is a canvas for creativity, compassion, and community. Unconventional online careers are a testament to the resilience of the human spirit, the power of empathy, and the profound impact of connection. This book invites you to explore, learn, and embrace the future, for in the world of unconventional online careers, the possibilities are as vast as the digital universe itself.

Introduction

Welcome to the brave new world of unconventional online jobs, where the boundaries of traditional employment blur into a pixelated playground of limitless possibilities. If you've ever daydreamed about turning your passion for virtual travel into a paycheck, providing a listening ear to those in need, or even becoming a professional virtual party planner, then this book is your ticket to the extraordinary.

In a time when we've collectively learned that remote work doesn't mean just trading pajama pants for office attire waist-up, the internet has opened doors to a realm of unique and sometimes downright quirky job opportunities. Gone are the days when a "real job" meant a desk in a brick-and-mortar office. Today, your office can be anywhere you want it to be, from a cozy corner of your living room to the bustling streets of a city halfway across the world.

In these pages, we'll embark on a digital adventure, uncovering careers that defy convention, spark curiosity, and redefine what "work" truly means. We'll meet the digital nomads who've turned wanderlust into a thriving business, the empathetic souls who lend an online ear, and the virtual party planners who make remote celebrations feel like a blast.

But this book isn't just about the cool and quirky—it's about empowering you to navigate the ever-evolving landscape of online work. Whether you're a seasoned remote worker looking for fresh inspiration or someone curious about taking their passions online, we've got you covered.

So, grab your favorite virtual coffee mug, get comfy in your home office (or couch), and let's dive headfirst into a world of unconventional online jobs that may just be your next big adventure. Your journey to digital success begins here.

Chapter 1: Virtual Friend or Companion

Imagine this: A cozy evening, your favorite blanket, a cup of tea, and your laptop. You're chatting away with someone who makes you laugh, listens to your day's stories, and genuinely cares about how you're feeling. Sounds like a typical hangout with a friend, right? Well, in today's digital age, it's not just friends you can hang out with; it's virtual friends or companions. And yes, people are actually willing to pay for it. You might be wondering, "Why on earth would anyone pay for online friendship?" Well, let's dive into this fascinating world and explore why virtual companionship is more than just a fleeting trend—it's a lifeline for many.

The Loneliness Epidemic

Loneliness isn't a new problem, but it's one that has become alarmingly prevalent in our hyper-connected world. Despite being surrounded by digital friends, social media, and chat apps, the feeling of isolation persists. People are craving something deeper, something more meaningful than endless scroll sessions and Instagram likes.

Cue virtual companions. In a world where physical proximity isn't always possible, especially for those who are geographically distant from loved ones, virtual friends fill that gap. They become your sounding board, your confidant, and your support system, all accessible through the click of a button.

Meet Sarah, a virtual friend and companion who embodies the essence of empathy and connection in the digital age. By day, she's a dedicated professional, managing her responsibilities with precision and grace. However, when she steps into the virtual world of companionship, Sarah transforms into a beacon of support, understanding, and friendship.

1. Building Meaningful Connections: Sarah's journey as a virtual friend begins with building genuine connections with individuals seeking companionship. Through text chats, video calls, or voice messages, she creates a warm and welcoming atmosphere where people can be themselves and share their thoughts, feelings, and experiences.

2. Offering a Listening Ear: Sarah excels in the art of active listening. She listens attentively to her companions, allowing them to express their joys, concerns, and challenges without judgment. Her empathetic responses and thoughtful questions make her companions feel heard and valued.

3. Providing Emotional Support: Sarah offers emotional support to those who may be going through difficult times. Whether it's a personal crisis, loneliness, or a need for guidance, she provides a comforting presence and encourages her companions to navigate their emotions and challenges with resilience.

4. Celebrating Life's Moments: Sarah rejoices in her companions' triumphs and joys, no matter how big or small. She celebrates birthdays, achievements, and milestones, bringing a sense of festivity and companionship to these special moments.

5. Engaging in Shared Interests: To deepen connections, Sarah explores shared interests with her companions. Whether it's discussing favorite books, movies, hobbies, or travel experiences, she creates opportunities for engaging conversations that foster a sense of camaraderie.

6. Offering Encouragement and Positivity: Sarah is an unwavering source of encouragement and positivity. She uplifts her companions' spirits when they are feeling down and provides motivation for pursuing their goals and dreams.

7. Respecting Boundaries: Sarah understands the importance of respecting boundaries. She ensures that her companions' comfort levels are paramount and never pushes them to share more than they are comfortable with.

8. Fostering a Supportive Community: Sarah also creates virtual spaces where her companions can connect with each other, fostering a supportive community of like-minded individuals who share their journey of seeking companionship and connection.

9. Multifaceted Connections: Whether it's being a friendly ear for casual conversation, a source of solace during challenging times, or a virtual cheerleader for personal goals, Sarah adapts her role to meet the unique needs of each companion.

Through Sarah's unwavering dedication and genuine compassion, she not only offers companionship but also creates a digital haven where individuals can find solace, understanding, and a true friend in times of need. In a world where physical proximity isn't always possible, Sarah's virtual companionship transcends distance, reminding us of the profound connections that can be forged through empathy, kindness, and the willingness to be there for one another.

Perhaps surprisingly, virtual companionship often feels more authentic than some face-to-face interactions. When you're connecting with someone online, there's often a level of anonymity and vulnerability that allows for deeper conversations. You're not bound by social norms or geographical constraints. You can be yourself, unfiltered and unapologetically.

And that's where the magic happens. Virtual companionship isn't just about chit-chatting; it's about forming genuine connections. You can explore shared interests, talk about life's ups and downs, or simply enjoy a good laugh together. It's like having a friend who's always there, ready to brighten your day.

When Virtual Companionship Matters

Now, you might be wondering who seeks out virtual friends, and why they'd be willing to pay for it. Well, the reasons are as diverse as the people themselves. Imagine:

1. *A student studying abroad, far from home, yearning for familiar conversations.*
2. *A retiree with an empty nest, looking to fill their days with companionship.*
3. *Someone grappling with mental health issues, seeking a non-judgmental listening ear.*
4. *An introvert who finds it easier to open up online than in person.*

5. *Individuals navigating major life changes, like divorce or a career shift, craving emotional support.*

These are just a few scenarios where virtual companionship becomes a lifeline. It's a way to combat loneliness, find solace, and create meaningful connections, even in a digital world. So, whether you're considering becoming a virtual companion or you're simply intrigued by this unconventional online job, you're about to embark on a journey that explores the beauty of human connection in the digital age. Virtual friendship—it's not just a trend; it's a lifeline for those in need.

Requirements to Become a Virtual Companion

1. **Strong Communication Skills**: Effective communication is key. You should be a good listener, empathetic, and capable of engaging in meaningful conversations.
2. **Reliability and Availability:** Clients might reach out to you at various times, so being dependable and having flexible availability is crucial.
3. **Tech Savvy:** You'll need a stable internet connection, a reliable device (like a computer or smartphone), and familiarity with video calling or chat apps.
4. **Empathy and Patience:** You'll often be supporting individuals who are going through tough times, so having empathy and patience is essential.
5. **Professionalism:** Maintain professionalism and respect client boundaries. Virtual companionship is a supportive role, so understanding your responsibilities is crucial.
6. **Established Online Presence:** Creating a professional online presence, such as a website or social media profiles, can help potential clients find and trust you.

Potential Earnings

The hourly rate for virtual companionship services can vary widely depending on factors like experience, specialization, and the demand for your services. However, to provide a ballpark figure, consider a range of $20 to $50 per hour.

Entry-level companions: Those new to the field or offering basic chat services might start at around $20 per hour.

Experienced companions: Individuals with several years of experience, excellent client reviews, or specialized skills (e.g., mental health support) might charge $30 to $50 per hour or more.

Keep in mind that the actual earnings can vary based on numerous factors, including your marketing efforts, the niche you serve, and the level of demand for your services. As you gain experience and build a positive reputation, you can potentially increase your rates over time.

Conclusion

In conclusion, embarking on a virtual companionship career can be a rewarding endeavor. It not only offers the opportunity to earn a reasonable income but also allows you to make a meaningful impact on the lives of those seeking emotional support and connection in the digital age. So, whether you're a stay-at-home mom looking to add fulfillment to your daily routine or a passionate communicator ready to embrace the role of a virtual friend, the requirements are within reach, and the potential earnings are promising. Your journey as a virtual companion begins here, with the possibility of touching lives and brightening days through the magic of digital connection.

For stay-at-home moms, this endeavor offers an exciting opportunity to venture beyond the familiar walls of home life. As you balance the duties of parenthood, you can also embrace the role of a virtual friend, sharing stories, laughter, and genuine connections with people from around the world. It's a chance to nurture your own passions and curiosities while making a meaningful impact on someone else's life. For those who find solace in connecting with others, whether you're an extrovert at heart or simply enjoy the warmth of human companionship, becoming a virtual companion might just be your calling. It's an avenue to extend your circle of friendship and provide vital emotional support to those who need it most.

So, whether you're a stay-at-home mom looking to add a dash of adventure to your daily routine or someone who thrives on the connections you forge with others, the world of virtual companionship beckons. It's a world where the ordinary becomes extraordinary, where human connection transcends borders and screens, and where the magic of friendship awaits your embrace.

In the chapters to come, we'll continue to explore unconventional online jobs that offer not only financial rewards but also the profound satisfaction of making a difference in people's lives. Virtual friendship—it's a journey that starts with a single click, but it's a journey that can lead to heartwarming stories, lifelong connections, and the fulfillment of bringing light into someone's day. Are you ready to embark on this adventure? The digital world awaits your friendly presence.

Chapter 2: Online Dating Profile Consultant

In a world where swipes replace first glances and chat bubbles stand in for romantic serenades, the quest for love has found a new digital stage. Welcome to the realm of online dating, where algorithms and profile pictures play matchmakers. But what if I told you that behind some of those captivating profiles lie the magic touch of an online dating profile consultant?

In this chapter, we'll delve into the enchanting world of those who specialize in making online dating dreams come true. They are the wizards of words, the maestros of photos, and the champions of swipe-worthy profiles. Their mission? To help individuals navigate the complexities of online dating and present themselves in the best possible light.

The Online Dating Conundrum

Let's face it: the world of online dating can be bewildering. Crafting the perfect profile that captures your essence while standing out in a sea of profiles isn't easy. That's where online dating profile consultants step in.

Picture this: Lisa, a vibrant and accomplished professional in her early thirties, was determined to find love in the digital age. Her career was soaring, her friends were happily settled, and the time felt right to explore the world of online dating. However, despite her many qualities and best intentions, her online dating profile seemed to be casting a spell of invisibility rather than attraction. As Lisa ventured into the world of online dating, she soon discovered that crafting the perfect profile was no easy feat. Her attempts at self-presentation, while genuine, fell short in capturing the attention of potential matches. Here's where her struggles lay:

Photo Puzzles: Lisa was genuinely baffled by the photo selection process. She had a collection of snapshots that captured her smiling at various social events, hiking in picturesque landscapes, and even enjoying quiet moments with her beloved cat. Yet, she couldn't quite figure out which pictures would showcase her personality best. Were her outdoor adventure photos too intimidating? Did her cat selfies make her seem too introverted? The uncertainty left her paralyzed, and she ended up selecting photos that she thought were safe but didn't necessarily stand out.

Bio Blockade: Lisa's bio was another puzzle she couldn't quite solve. She knew that her professional accomplishments were significant and important to her identity, but they seemed to overshadow the playful and adventurous side of her personality. As she attempted to convey her ambition and drive, she struggled to balance it with her love for spontaneous road trips and painting sessions. Crafting a bio that was both impressive and relatable was a challenge that had her editing and re-editing her profile text until it felt generic and uninspiring.

Message Muddle: The complexities of online dating etiquette were yet another hurdle for Lisa. When it came to initiating conversations and maintaining engaging dialogues, she often found herself at a loss. The fear of coming across as too eager or too distant led to messages that felt forced and formulaic. Her attempts at meaningful conversations sometimes veered into awkward territory, causing promising connections to fizzle out.

As weeks turned into months, Lisa's frustration grew. The excitement of online dating had given way to a sense of discouragement and contemplation of giving up on her quest for love in the digital age. It was at this crucial juncture that she discovered the world of online dating profile consultants, experts who possessed the key to unlock the potential of her profile and breathe life into her digital persona.

Then, Lisa stumbled upon the world of online dating profile consultants. With a few clicks, she connected with Sarah, a dating profile guru who possessed a unique knack for transforming ordinary profiles into magnetic masterpieces. Sarah not only helped Lisa choose the perfect profile picture but also crafted a bio that highlighted her charm, wit, and authenticity. The result? Lisa's inbox filled with messages from intriguing, like-minded individuals genuinely interested in getting to know her. She found herself on engaging dates, building connections that felt genuine and promising—all thanks to the expert guidance of her online dating profile consultant.

The Art and Science of Profile Optimization

Creating an enticing online dating profile is both an art and a science. Online dating profile consultants understand the nuances of this delicate dance. They consider factors like tone, authenticity, and visual appeal to help clients put their best virtual foot forward.

1. **Photo Selection:** Consultants advise on the choice of profile pictures, emphasizing the importance of clear, high-quality images that showcase personality and interests. The goal is to invite curiosity and convey authenticity.

2. **Bio Crafting:** Consultants are wordsmiths, skillfully weaving words to create profiles that reflect each individual's unique story. They help clients strike the right balance between vulnerability and intrigue, inviting potential matches to discover more.

3. **Messaging Strategies:** Beyond profile optimization, consultants guide clients on messaging strategies. They offer tips on initiating conversations, maintaining engaging dialogues, and transitioning from digital connections to real-life dates.

Why Seek Professional Help?

In a fast-paced world where first impressions are formed in seconds, an optimized online dating profile can be the key to finding meaningful connections. People turn to online dating profile consultants for various reasons:

1. *Lack of Time: Busy professionals often lack the time to fine-tune their profiles, making professional assistance invaluable.*

2. *Profile Fatigue: After numerous unsuccessful attempts, some individuals grow weary of the trial-and-error process and seek expert guidance.*
3. *Confidence Boost: Consultants provide a confidence boost, helping clients recognize and embrace their unique qualities.*
4. *Increased Success: Ultimately, hiring a consultant can lead to more successful matches and meaningful connections.*

Potential Earnings

The earnings of online dating profile consultants can vary depending on their experience, reputation, and the level of demand for their services. Here's a breakdown:

Entry-Level Consultants: Those new to the field may charge around $30 to $50 per hour for their services.

Experienced Consultants: Professionals with a strong track record and a portfolio of successful profiles might command rates of $50 to $100 per hour or more.

Conclusion

As we navigate the uncharted waters of online dating, the role of online dating profile consultants becomes increasingly vital. They are the modern-day Cupids, armed not with bows and arrows but with words, images, and strategies that breathe life into digital profiles. And in doing so, they bring countless love stories to life—one swipe at a time.

So, whether you're a hopeful romantic looking for love in the digital age or someone with a passion for words and human connections, the world of online dating profile consultancy awaits. It's a world where words weave love stories, photos paint personality portraits, and the journey to find love online becomes an art form in itself. Dive in, and let the adventure begin.

Chapter 3: Online Listening or Venting Service

In the bustling chaos of our modern lives, where the digital realm often acts as both a sanctuary and a stressor, there emerges an oasis of empathetic support—a unique service that offers solace through the simple act of listening. This is the world of online listening or venting services, where people can pour out their hearts, share their thoughts, and find a compassionate ear on the other end of the line.

The Weight of Unspoken Words

Nancy was, by all outward appearances, a high-achieving dynamo. Her career trajectory was on a rapid ascent, she had a loving family, and a circle of friends who admired her for her unwavering determination. Yet, beneath this facade of success, Nancy bore the weight of unspoken thoughts and emotions that threatened to engulf her.

At work, the demands seemed relentless. Long hours at the office and the pressure to meet ambitious targets took a toll on her physical and mental well-being. Nancy had always been driven, but now the drive was spiraling into a ceaseless cycle of perfectionism. She found herself revisiting conversations and decisions, questioning her choices long after others had moved on. The fear of failure, of letting down her team, consumed her thoughts like a relentless storm.

In her personal life, the juggling act was equally relentless. As a devoted wife and mother, Nancy strived to be present for her family. However, the mental load of coordinating schedules; managing household chores, and ensuring her children's well-being became a never-ending reel of responsibilities. The quiet moments of reflection she once cherished had vanished, replaced by a ceaseless stream of mental to-do lists.

The impact of this unrelenting inner turmoil was profound. Nancy's sleep, once restful, now eluded her. Nights became a battlefield of anxious thoughts and racing heartbeats. She would often lie awake, replaying her day, scrutinizing her choices, and fearing the challenges that tomorrow would bring.

Her social life suffered too. Nancy withdrew from friends and family, unable to articulate the storm raging within her. She feared burdening them with her struggles, fearing they wouldn't understand the pressure she placed on herself. Loneliness crept into her life, even in the midst of a crowd. Amid these sleepless nights and isolated days, Nancy came to a stark realization—she needed an outlet, a way to unburden her heart and mind. She needed someone who could listen without judgment, without offering solutions, and simply allow her to vent her thoughts, her fears, and her frustrations.

It was during one of these late-night Google searches that Nancy discovered the concept of online listening or venting services. In this digital sanctuary, she found solace—a place where she could pour out her heart without fear, knowing that there was someone on the other end, a trained listener, ready to offer a compassionate and non-judgmental ear.

A Listening Ear in a Noisy World

Online listening or venting services cater to individuals like Nancy, who yearn for an outlet to unload their emotional baggage. The beauty of these services lies in their simplicity: clients can pour out their hearts without fear of judgment or the need for solutions. It's about being heard and acknowledged, about finding relief in knowing that someone cares enough to listen.

These services often involve trained listeners who excel in the art of active listening. They offer a non-judgmental, compassionate presence that allows clients to vent their frustrations, share their joys, or simply talk through their thoughts and feelings. It's a form of emotional catharsis in the digital age, where the boundaries of time and space fade away, leaving only the human connection.

Why Seek an Online Listening Service?

The need for online listening or venting services stems from a variety of circumstances: Isolation: Some individuals may feel isolated, lacking a support system or a confidant they can turn to.

1. *Anonymity: Online platforms offer a level of anonymity that allows people to speak freely about deeply personal issues they might not be comfortable discussing with those they know.*

2. *Emotional Release: Sharing one's thoughts and emotions can be therapeutic, providing relief from the weight of unresolved feelings.*

3. *Non-judgmental Support: These services offer a judgment-free zone where clients can express themselves without fear of criticism or advice they might not be ready to accept.*

Becoming a virtual listener, also known as an online listener or venting service provider, involves a commitment to offering empathetic support and a safe space for individuals to share their thoughts and emotions. While there are no specific formal qualifications, there are essential requirements and skills you should possess to excel in this role:

The Requirements to Become a Virtual listener

Empathy: Empathy is at the core of being an effective virtual listener. You need to genuinely care about the well-being of the people you're listening to and be able to understand and share their feelings.

Active Listening Skills: Active listening involves not only hearing the words but also understanding the emotions and nuances behind them. It's about giving your full attention, asking clarifying questions when necessary, and providing thoughtful responses.

Non-judgmental Attitude: It's crucial to approach every conversation with an open, non-judgmental mindset. People seeking your services often share personal and sensitive information, and they need to feel safe doing so.

Patience: You may encounter clients who are distressed, anxious, or struggling with complex emotions. Patience is essential as you allow them to express themselves at their own pace.

Excellent Communication Skills: While you don't need to provide solutions or advice, you should be able to communicate effectively and convey understanding and empathy through your responses.

Cultural Sensitivity: Virtual listeners often interact with a diverse range of clients from various cultural backgrounds. Being culturally sensitive and aware of potential differences in communication styles and values is important.

Confidentiality: Maintaining client confidentiality is paramount. Clients need to trust that their conversations will remain private and not be shared with others.

Boundaries: Setting and maintaining clear boundaries is crucial. You should be able to recognize when a client's needs may exceed the scope of your role and direct them to appropriate resources when necessary.

Training and Education: While there's no formal education required, some training in active listening and communication skills can be beneficial. Many organizations offer online courses and resources on active listening and providing emotional support.

Reliable Internet and Communication Tools: As a virtual listener, you'll need a stable internet connection and access to communication tools like video calls, chat platforms, or phone services to connect with clients.

Availability: Being available during scheduled listening sessions is important. You may need to work flexible hours to accommodate clients' needs.

Compassion: Beyond empathy, genuine compassion for the well-being of others is a driving force in this role. You should be motivated by the desire to help and support those in need.

Self-Care: Listening to people's emotional struggles can be emotionally taxing. Practicing self-care and knowing when to seek support for yourself is vital to prevent burnout.

Potential Earnings

The earnings of virtual listeners can vary based on factors such as experience, specialization, and the platform or organization they work with. Here's a rough estimate of potential earnings:

Entry-Level Listeners: Those new to the field or offering basic listening services might start at around $15 to $30 per hour.

Experienced Listeners: As you gain experience and build a positive reputation, you can potentially charge $30 to $50 per hour or more.

Specialized Listeners: Some virtual listeners specialize in specific areas, such as grief counseling or mental health support. These specialists may command higher rates, ranging from $50 to $100 per hour or more, depending on their expertise.

Please note that these figures can vary widely based on factors like geographic location, the demand for your services, and your ability to effectively market yourself. Additionally, some virtual listeners may choose to offer their services on a subscription or package basis, providing clients with a certain number of listening sessions for a fixed fee.

Conclusion

As you establish your practice and gain experience, you can adjust your rates to reflect your expertise and the value you provide to clients. It's essential to research industry standards and pricing in your area to ensure your rates are competitive while also reflecting the quality of service you offer.

As we navigate the intricacies of our fast-paced lives, online listening or venting services emerge as a beacon of emotional support. They offer a space where silence can be as comforting as words, and where empathy flows through the digital waves.

Chapter 4: Digital Confidant for Secrets

In a world where the pace of life seems to quicken with each passing day, and the line between our public selves and our private thoughts blurs, there exists a unique and profound service—a sanctuary for the unspoken burdens we carry. Welcome to the realm of the digital confidant for secrets, where individuals can anonymously share their deepest confessions, fears, and guilt with a compassionate listener who offers emotional support and unwavering confidentiality.

The Weight of Unspoken Secrets

David, a middle-aged man with a mop of salt-and-pepper hair, had always projected an image of calm and composure. To the world, he was a symbol of stability and reliability, a loving husband and father, and a respected member of his community. However, behind this facade of normalcy lurked a secret that had festered within him for years, a secret that had taken an insidious toll on his psychological well-being.

In the quiet moments of David's life, when the world faded into the background and he was left alone with his thoughts, guilt gnawed at his conscience like an unrelenting adversary. It was a guilt born of choices made long ago, choices that had seemed insignificant at the time but had since grown into a formidable presence in his mind. The guilt had a way of seeping into his every waking moment. Amidst the mundane routines of daily life, it whispered in his ear, reminding him of the moral ambiguity of his actions. It invaded his dreams, turning nights of rest into turbulent landscapes of regret and anxiety. His once-clear conscience now felt like a murky pool, clouded by the unresolved issue he carried.

David yearned to unburden his soul, to confess his secret and seek solace in the release of his guilt. Yet, the fear of judgment, of the repercussions his revelation might bring, kept him silent. He couldn't confide in his loving wife, fearing the damage it might do to their relationship. His friends and colleagues saw him as a pillar of strength; he couldn't bear the thought of shattering that image. So, he carried the weight alone, and it grew heavier with each passing day.

It was during one of his lowest moments, when he sat in the dim glow of his computer screen, that he found a glimmer of hope. David had stumbled upon an online forum where individuals could share their deepest secrets anonymously. The idea of unburdening himself to a faceless, understanding stranger was intriguing. He mustered the courage to type out his secret, his fingers trembling over the keyboard.

To his surprise, the response he received was not one of condemnation but of empathy and support. A kind and understanding individual had reached out to him, offering a listening ear without judgment. David poured out his heart, confessing the secret that had haunted him for years. It was a moment of release, a catharsis he hadn't dared to hope for.

This newfound connection, this digital friendship, changed something within David. The weight of his secret no longer felt insurmountable. He realized that he wasn't alone in his struggle and that there were others who carried their burdens in silence. He partnered with his online confidant to create a space where people could unburden themselves anonymously, free from the fear of judgment and consequences. Together, they became digital confidants, offering solace and understanding to those who, like David, carried secrets that weighed heavily on their hearts.

The Power of Anonymous Catharsis

In the realm of digital confidants for secrets, individuals like David find solace. They can anonymously share their most intimate thoughts and confessions with a compassionate and trustworthy listener. It's a safe space where the burden of secrecy can be gently lifted, where guilt and shame can be replaced with understanding and empathy.

People may want to confide a wide range of intimate thoughts and confessions when seeking the services of digital confidants. Here are some examples:

Relationship Struggles: *Sharing doubts, fears, and concerns about their romantic relationships, including issues with communication, trust, or infidelity.*

Personal Regrets: *Confessing past mistakes or regrets, such as decisions that led to negative consequences or actions they wish they could take back.*

Family Conflicts: *Discussing conflicts and challenges within their family dynamics, including estrangements, disagreements, or feelings of guilt related to family members.*

Career Anxieties: *Voicing concerns about their professional life, such as job-related stress, dissatisfaction, or fears of job loss.*

Secret Passions: *Sharing hidden interests, hobbies, or passions that they haven't felt comfortable revealing to others.*

Mental Health Struggles: *Discussing issues related to mental health, such as anxiety, depression, self-esteem issues, or thoughts of self-harm.*

Financial Concerns: *Confessing financial troubles, including debt, overspending, or financial mistakes that have impacted their well-being.*

Loss and Grief: *Opening up about the pain of losing a loved one, grief, or the lingering emotions related to a past loss.*

Life Goals and Dreams: *Discussing unfulfilled dreams, aspirations, and ambitions that they've been hesitant to pursue.*

Identity and Self-Discovery: *Sharing personal struggles related to identity, self-acceptance, and self-discovery, including issues related to sexuality or gender.*

Addictions: *Confiding in struggles with addiction, whether it's related to substances, gambling, or other compulsive behaviors.*

Secret Crushes: *Discussing feelings for someone they're not in a relationship with, sometimes leading to infidelity or confusion.*

Moral Dilemmas: *Exploring ethical or moral dilemmas they're facing and seeking guidance on how to navigate them.*

Past Trauma: *Revealing past traumatic experiences or abuse that they've never spoken about to anyone.*

Insecurities: *Discussing deep-seated insecurities or self-doubts that affect their self-esteem and well-being.*

Existential Questions: *Sharing philosophical or existential questions about the purpose of life, spirituality, or the nature of existence.*

These examples illustrate the breadth and depth of the intimate thoughts and confessions people may carry with them. The role of a digital confidant is to provide a safe, non-judgmental space for individuals to share these thoughts and feelings, offering understanding and emotional support to help them unburden their hearts and find a sense of relief.

The appeal of this service lies in its anonymity and non-judgmental support. Clients can unburden themselves without revealing their identity, freeing them from the fear of social consequences or personal condemnation. The digital confidant is a silent partner in their journey, providing emotional support and validation without offering solutions or advice unless explicitly requested.

Why Seek a Digital Confidant for Secrets?

People turn to digital confidants for secrets for various reasons:

1. *Anonymity: Anonymity allows clients to share deeply personal or potentially stigmatized information without fear of exposure.*

2. *Catharsis: Confession and sharing can be inherently therapeutic, providing relief from the weight of unspoken secrets.*
3. *Emotional Support: Clients seek emotional support and understanding from a non-judgmental listener who can offer validation and empathy.*
4. *Maintaining Relationships: For some, the service helps preserve existing relationships by allowing them to unburden themselves without directly involving loved ones.*

The Requirements to Become a Digital Confidant

Becoming a digital confidant for secrets requires specific qualities and skills:

Empathy: The ability to empathize with clients' emotions without judgment is paramount.

Non-Judgmental Attitude: A commitment to maintaining strict confidentiality and refraining from offering unsolicited advice or opinions.

Active Listening Skills: Effective listening skills are crucial for understanding and responding to clients' confessions.

Patience: Clients may struggle to articulate their thoughts or emotions, requiring patience and understanding.

Communication Skills: While the role involves listening, clear and respectful communication is essential.

Potential Earnings

Earnings for digital confidants can vary widely depending on experience and reputation:

Entry-Level Confidants: Those new to the field might start at around $20 to $40 per hour.

Experienced Confidants: With experience and positive reviews, earnings can range from $40 to $80 per hour or more.

Specialized Confidants: Some may specialize in certain areas, such as grief counseling or relationship issues, and command higher rates.

Conclusion

In the digital age, where secrets are both shared and guarded with unprecedented complexity, the role of the digital confidant for secrets is one of quiet support, compassion, and anonymity. It's a testament to the human need to unburden the soul, to seek understanding, and to find solace in the faceless confessional of cyberspace. As we continue to explore unconventional online jobs, this chapter reveals that even the most deeply concealed secrets can find release in the digital world, and that compassionate listeners stand ready to provide the support and understanding that clients seek.

Chapter 5: Online Personal Historian

In the rich tapestry of unconventional online careers, the role of the online personal historian emerges as a guardian of memories and narratives. These dedicated individuals collaborate with clients to document their life stories, family histories, or personal memoirs. Through interviews, research, and creative storytelling, they craft written or multimedia narratives that capture the essence of a person's journey, ensuring that these cherished stories endure for future generations.

The Essence of an Online Personal Historian

Meet Robert, an online personal historian who weaves the threads of lives into captivating narratives. By day, he''s a teacher, imparting knowledge to young minds. However, when his virtual interview space opens, Robert transforms into a custodian of stories, diligently recording the experiences and wisdom of his clients.

Robert's journey as an online personal historian is a testament to his deep reverence for stories, a commitment to preserving legacies, and a passion for the art of storytelling. When he steps into his virtual interview space, it's as if he enters a sacred realm where the stories of individuals and families come to life.

1. Establishing Trust and Connection: Robert's process begins with building a strong rapport with his clients. He understands that the act of sharing one's life story is a deeply personal experience. Through warm and empathetic conversations, he creates a safe and inviting atmosphere where clients feel comfortable sharing their memories.

2. Conducting Meaningful Interviews: Robert is a skilled interviewer, adept at asking probing questions that elicit insightful narratives. He guides his clients through their life journeys, coaxing out the vivid details, anecdotes, and emotions that shape their stories. He listens not just to the words but to the emotions and nuances behind them.

3. Thorough Research: To provide historical context and accuracy to the narratives, Robert delves into extensive research. He scours family records, photographs, letters, and documents, piecing together the puzzle of his clients' lives. This meticulous research ensures that the stories he creates are rich and authentic.

4. Crafting Engaging Narratives: With a blend of journalistic acumen and creative storytelling, Robert brings these collected stories to life. He meticulously crafts written narratives that captivate readers or viewers, preserving the essence of the individuals he profiles. His narratives are not just chronological accounts but vibrant and emotionally resonant tales.

5. Multimedia Expertise: For clients who prefer multimedia narratives, Robert utilizes his expertise in video editing, audio production, and graphic design. He combines visuals, music, and voiceovers to create compelling video or audio documentaries that enhance the storytelling experience.

6. Preservation and Sharing: Once the narratives are complete, Robert ensures that they are preserved for future generations. He helps clients decide on the most suitable format for their stories, whether it's a beautifully bound book, a digital archive, or a multimedia presentation. This ensures that the wisdom and experiences of his clients endure.

7. Emotional Support: Robert understands that the process of recounting life stories can be emotionally charged. He offers gentle guidance and emotional support throughout the journey, helping clients navigate the memories and reflections that surface during the interviews.

8. Celebrating Legacies: Perhaps one of the most rewarding aspects of Robert's role is witnessing the joy and fulfillment in his clients' eyes when they see their stories transformed into timeless legacies. He celebrates with them, recognizing that he has not only documented their past but also illuminated their significance in the grand tapestry of human history.

Through Robert's unwavering dedication and passion for storytelling, he ensures that the narratives of his clients are not lost to time. He is a custodian of stories, a bridge between generations, and a guardian of the wisdom, experiences, and legacies that define individuals and families. Robert's virtual interview space becomes a vessel through which stories are preserved, cherished, and shared, allowing them to resonate with future generations in the ongoing journey of the human experience.

The Significance of Personal Histories

The allure of online personal historians lies in their ability to create enduring legacies:

1. *Interviewing and Listening: They engage in deep, empathetic conversations with clients, coaxing out cherished memories, life lessons, and untold stories. Through active listening, they uncover the richness of personal experiences.*

2. *Research and Compilation: Personal historians conduct thorough research to provide context and historical accuracy to the narratives. They delve into family archives, documents, photographs, and other records to piece together the puzzle of a person's life.*

3. *Creative Storytelling: Armed with a blend of journalism and storytelling skills, they craft written or multimedia narratives that captivate readers or viewers. These narratives breathe life into the stories they've collected, allowing the essence of the individual to shine through.*

4. *Preservation for Future Generations: The stories created by online personal historians become cherished heirlooms, passed down through generations. They serve as a bridge connecting past, present, and future, ensuring that the wisdom and experiences of ancestors are never lost.*

The Requirements

Becoming an online personal historian demands a combination of qualities and skills:

Empathy: The ability to connect with clients on a deep emotional level is crucial. Personal historians must create a safe space where individuals feel comfortable sharing their life stories.

Interviewing Skills: Effective interviewing techniques are essential to elicit meaningful and insightful narratives from clients.

Research Acumen: Proficiency in research methods and historical context ensures the accuracy and authenticity of the narratives.

Writing and Storytelling: Strong writing skills and a knack for creative storytelling are vital for crafting compelling narratives.

Multimedia Skills: For those who create multimedia narratives, proficiency in video editing, audio production, and graphic design may be necessary.

Potential Earnings

Earnings for online personal historians can vary based on factors like experience, the scope of projects, and the demand for their services:

Entry-Level Historians: Beginners may charge around $20 to $50 per hour of work on a project.

Experienced Historians: With growing expertise and a portfolio of completed projects, historians can potentially earn between $50 and $100 or more per hour.

Specialized Historians: Those who specialize in niche areas or offer unique storytelling approaches may command higher rates.

Conclusion

In the digital age, where the pace of life often obscures the significance of personal stories, online personal historians stand as guardians of memories and wisdom. They immortalize the narratives that define individuals and families, bridging generations and ensuring that the legacy of lives lived is never forgotten. As we delve into unconventional online careers, this chapter unveils the remarkable role of online personal historians and their ability to transform memories into timeless treasures, connecting past, present, and future in a tapestry of human experience.

Chapter 6: Virtual Storyteller

In the enchanting realm of virtual storytelling, a unique and heartwarming occupation thrives—the virtual storyteller. These gifted individuals possess the artistry to craft and narrate personalized stories that serve as bedtime tales for children, special gifts for loved ones, or even as therapeutic tools to help individuals relax and conquer life's challenges.

The Magic of Virtual Storytelling

Imagine meeting Sarah, a virtual storyteller with an extraordinary gift for weaving enchanting narratives. By day, she was a dedicated teacher, nurturing young minds with knowledge and wisdom. But when the sun dipped below the horizon and the world embraced the embrace of night, Sarah transformed into a storyteller of dreams.

Through the soft glow of her computer screen, Sarah ventures into realms of imagination where she could bring stories to life. Her tales traverse through enchanted forests, soar to the stars, and whisper secrets of bravery and kindness into the hearts of her listeners. Sarah knows that stories possess the power to heal, inspire, and transport her audience to places where their own dreams could flourish.

In the quiet moments before bedtime, as little ones nestle beneath their covers, their wide-eyed anticipation creates a magical atmosphere that Sarah cherishes. Her stories are carefully crafted to transport her young listeners to enchanted forests where talking animals imparted wisdom, to galaxies where stars danced in cosmic ballets, and to realms where the courage of heroes shone brightly.

Within her stories, Sarah whispers secrets of bravery and kindness, the very qualities she believes could shape young hearts and minds. She knows that stories have the remarkable power to heal, inspire, and transport her audience to places where their own dreams could flourish. For Sarah, each bedtime tale is a labor of love, a creation spun from the threads of her imagination, and a gift she offers to parents and children alike. She understands the importance of creating not just stories but cherishes memories that families would carry with them throughout their lives.

In the tapestry of her narratives, Sarah weaves bonds of closeness between parents and their children. Her stories become a cherished tradition, a nightly ritual where families gather, hearts entwined in the magic of storytelling. As she narrates tales of adventure, courage, and wonder, parents watch their children's faces light up with delight, and children feel the warmth of their parents' love in the tender embrace of storytelling.

Sarah's specialization in bedtime stories goes beyond creating captivating tales; it is about fostering connections and nurturing the belief that, within the pages of a story, anything is possible. Through her dedication and the gentle cadence of her storytelling, she helps families find solace in the tranquility of the evening, find courage in the face of darkness, and find dreams that would carry them through the night, into a new day filled with hope and imagination.

The Versatility of Virtual Stories

The allure of virtual storytelling rests in its versatility and ability to touch lives in diverse ways:

1. *Bedtime Stories: For parents seeking to create magical bedtime rituals, virtual storytellers offer tales that whisk children away to dreamland, fostering a love for reading and the boundless wonders of the imagination.*

2. *Special Occasions: On anniversaries, birthdays, or special milestones, individuals turn to virtual storytellers to create personalized narratives that capture the essence of their cherished relationships or the journey of their loved ones.*

3. Therapeutic Storytelling: In the realm of therapeutic storytelling, virtual storytellers craft tales tailored to individuals dealing with anxiety, stress, or trauma. These stories serve as healing tools, providing solace, strength, and a pathway to resilience.

The Requirements to Become a Virtual Storyteller

Becoming a virtual storyteller involves a unique blend of creativity, empathy, and technical skills:

Creativity: Storytellers must possess a vivid imagination to conjure captivating plots, characters, and worlds that engage and enchant their audience.

Voice and Diction: The ability to narrate stories with clear and expressive vocal delivery is essential to create an immersive experience.

Empathy: To craft therapeutic stories, storytellers must empathize with their clients, understanding their struggles and tailoring narratives to address specific needs.

Technical Proficiency: Familiarity with audio recording and editing equipment/software is crucial to produce high-quality audio stories.

Potential Earnings

Earnings for virtual storytellers can vary depending on factors such as experience, specialization, and the demand for their services:

Beginner Storytellers: Those new to the field might start at around $20 to $50 per hour.

Experienced Storytellers: As storytellers gain experience and build a loyal client base, they can potentially earn in the range of $50 to $100 per hour or more.

Specialized Storytellers: Those who specialize in therapeutic storytelling or create highly personalized narratives may command higher rates.

Conclusion

In the realm of virtual storytelling, where words become the brushstrokes of imagination and healing, virtual storytellers are the custodians of dreams. They create tapestries of wonder and emotion, stitching together tales that spark laughter, soothe troubled souls, and kindle the flames of inspiration. As we journey through the world of unconventional online jobs, this chapter reveals the enchanting role of virtual storytellers and their capacity to touch hearts, one story at a time.

Chapter 7: Online Cultural Exchange Host

In the boundless expanse of the digital world, a remarkable occupation thrives—the online cultural exchange host. These skilled individuals serve as the architects of virtual bridges, connecting people from diverse corners of the globe and facilitating the exchange of cultures through engaging discussions, cooking sessions, language lessons, and interactive activities.

The Heart of Online Cultural Exchange

Carlos, the online cultural exchange host, is a testament to the power of passion and technology in bringing people from diverse backgrounds closer together. While his daytime role as a computer programmer delves into the intricacies of the digital realm, it is his fervor for exploring the world's cultures that truly ignites his spirit.

Global Conversations and Insights: Carlos's journey as an online cultural exchange host begins with meticulous research. He delves deep into the cultural nuances, traditions, and history of the regions he wishes to showcase. His goal is not just to provide superficial glimpses but to offer profound insights that foster genuine understanding.

Creating a Virtual Hub: Carlos meticulously plans and curates online sessions where participants from different corners of the globe can converge. He understands the significance of creating a welcoming virtual space where individuals feel comfortable sharing their cultures. This involves selecting suitable online platforms, arranging schedules to accommodate various time zones, and crafting invitations that exude warmth and inclusivity.

Facilitating Cross-Cultural Dialogues: Central to Carlos's mission are the cross-cultural dialogues he facilitates. He crafts thoughtful discussion topics that encourage participants to share their traditions, beliefs, and stories. These conversations transcend mere information exchange; they are opportunities for people to connect on a deeper level, fostering empathy and appreciation.

Culinary Adventures: In one of his sessions, Carlos might embark on a culinary adventure. He guides participants through the preparation of traditional dishes, sharing anecdotes about the ingredients' cultural significance. As kitchens buzz with activity worldwide, participants savor the flavors of distant lands, forging connections through shared culinary experiences.

Language Lessons: Language, as Carlos knows, is the key to unlocking a culture's heart. He offers language lessons, teaching participants basic phrases and expressions. As participants stumble over foreign words and share laughter in the process, barriers dissolve, and bonds strengthen.

Interactive Activities: Carlos believes that culture extends beyond language and food—it's also about art, music, dance, and more. He organizes interactive activities like dance lessons, art workshops, and music sessions. These immersive experiences allow participants to step into the shoes of another culture, celebrating the beauty of diversity.

Building Cultural Bridges: Through his work, Carlos becomes a bridge builder, connecting individuals who might have never crossed paths otherwise. He fosters understanding, dismantles stereotypes, and creates a space where appreciation for differences thrives.

Carlos's passion for cultural exchange isn't just about sharing knowledge; it's about cultivating empathy, respect, and friendship among participants. He knows that every session is a step toward a more connected and harmonious world, where diversity is not just celebrated but cherished. In the digital age, he is a harbinger of unity, an ambassador of cultural appreciation, and a true global citizen.

A World of Exchange

The appeal of online cultural exchange hosts lies in their ability to create diverse and enriching experiences:

1. *Global Conversations: These hosts facilitate cross-cultural dialogues, where individuals from different parts of the world come together to discuss topics such as traditions, customs, art, and daily life.*

2. *Culinary Adventures: Cooking sessions offer participants the chance to savor the flavors of distant lands. Hosts guide them through the preparation of traditional dishes, transforming kitchens into global culinary classrooms.*

3. *Language Lessons: Language is a gateway to culture. Online hosts provide language lessons, enabling participants to learn phrases and expressions that bridge linguistic divides.*

4. *Interactive Activities: Cultural exchange is brought to life through activities like dance lessons, art workshops, and music sessions, allowing participants to immerse themselves in new experiences.*

The Requirements

Becoming an online cultural exchange host requires a unique blend of skills and qualities:

Cultural Knowledge: Hosts should possess a deep understanding of their own culture as well as the cultures they aim to introduce, ensuring accuracy and authenticity in their interactions.

Communication Skills: Effective communication is essential for facilitating meaningful cross-cultural dialogues and activities.

Adaptability: Hosts must adapt to the needs and interests of their participants, creating engaging and personalized cultural experiences.

Tech Savvy: Proficiency in using online platforms for video conferencing, streaming, and collaboration is crucial.

Potential Earnings

Earnings for online cultural exchange hosts can vary depending on factors such as experience, specialization, and the demand for their services:

Entry-Level Hosts: Those starting out might earn modestly, ranging from $20 to $50 per hour.

Experienced Hosts: As hosts build a reputation and a loyal following, earnings can increase to several hundred dollars per hour.

Specialized Hosts: Those who specialize in unique cultural experiences may command higher rates.

Conclusion

In the age of digital connectivity, where the world's boundaries are blurred by the click of a button, online cultural exchange hosts are the bridge builders, the global storytellers, and the architects of understanding. They offer the world a chance to come together, to celebrate diversity, and to discover the beauty of cultural exchange. As we journey through the realm of unconventional online jobs, this chapter unveils the transformative role of online cultural exchange hosts and their ability to foster connections and mutual respect among people from different walks of life and corners of the world.

Chapter 8: Online Mealtime Companion

In the ever-expanding landscape of online jobs, a heartwarming and vital role thrives—the online mealtime companion. These compassionate individuals bridge the gap of solitude, sharing virtual dining tables with those who eat alone or crave companionship during their meals. Through video calls, they offer not just company but the warmth of engaging conversation, transforming ordinary meals into moments of connection.

The Essence of the Online Mealtime Companion

Meet Sofia, an online mealtime companion with a heart as generous as her smile. By profession, she's a freelance writer, crafting words that dance on the pages of novels. However, her true calling lies in the simple yet profound act of sharing meals with those who hunger not just for food but for human connection.

Sofia's mission as an online mealtime companion goes beyond the mere act of sharing a virtual meal; it's about crafting an experience that nourishes both the body and the soul of her clients. She approaches her role with genuine empathy, warmth, and a deep understanding of the significance of human connection.

1. Building Trust and Connection: Sofia begins by building a sense of trust and connection with her clients. She takes the time to get to know them, their preferences, and their unique backgrounds. This initial connection forms the foundation of a meaningful mealtime experience.

2. Creating a Comfortable Atmosphere: Before the meal begins, Sofia ensures that the virtual dining space is warm and inviting. She may adjust the lighting, choose a comfortable seating arrangement, and even set the mood with soft background music. Her goal is to make clients feel as though they are sharing a meal in the coziest of settings.

3. Thoughtful Menu Selection: Depending on the client's preferences, Sofia collaborates with them to select a menu that suits their tastes. Whether it's a home-cooked meal, takeout from a favorite restaurant, or even a themed culinary adventure, the menu is chosen with care to enhance the overall experience.

4. Engaging Conversation: As the meal unfolds, Sofia's gift for engaging conversation shines through. She is a skilled conversationalist, adept at steering discussions toward topics that resonate with her clients. These conversations can range from shared memories, interests, dreams, and even cultural exchanges.

5. Active Listening: One of Sofia's most cherished abilities is her knack for active listening. She not only hears her clients' words but also understands the unspoken emotions behind them. This deep level of empathy allows her to provide the emotional support and companionship that many crave during mealtime.

6. Celebrating Special Occasions: For clients celebrating birthdays, anniversaries, or other special occasions, Sofia goes the extra mile. She might surprise them with a personalized cake, decorations, or a virtual toast to mark the momentous event, ensuring that these milestones are cherished and celebrated.

7. Cultural Explorations: Sofia often incorporates cultural elements into her mealtime experiences. For instance, if her client is interested in Japanese culture, she may arrange for a sushi-making session or share interesting insights about Japan. This not only educates but also enriches the mealtime with cultural diversity.

8. Post-Meal Reflection: After the meal, Sofia encourages clients to reflect on the experience. This may include discussing their favorite parts of the meal, memorable moments from the conversation, or any new insights gained. These reflections solidify the bond created during the meal.

Sofia's approach to online mealtime companionship is a testament to the power of human connection. Through her unwavering dedication and thoughtful planning, she transforms solitary meals into celebrations of togetherness. Every bite shared with Sofia is a reminder that, even in a virtual world, the simple act of dining can be a source of warmth, camaraderie, and genuine human connection.

The Significance of Shared Meals

The allure of online mealtime companions lies in the transformative power of shared meals:

1. *A Sense of Community: In an increasingly isolated world, shared meals foster a sense of belonging and community. Individuals connect with companions who become friends, sharing stories, experiences, and laughter.*
2. *Reducing Loneliness: For those who might otherwise eat alone, online companions offer a lifeline against loneliness. The simple act of being seen and heard during meals eases the ache of solitude.*
3. *Cultural Exchange: Meals transcend borders, offering a window into different cultures. Online companions may come from diverse backgrounds, enriching conversations with cultural insights and culinary delights.*

Requirements

Becoming an online mealtime companion requires a unique blend of qualities and skills:

Empathy: The ability to connect with others emotionally and provide genuine companionship is paramount.

Communication Skills: Engaging in meaningful conversation and active listening are vital to creating a warm and welcoming mealtime environment.

Flexibility: Companions must adapt to the preferences and schedules of their clients, ensuring every mealtime experience is comfortable and enjoyable.

Tech Savvy: Proficiency in video conferencing platforms and a stable internet connection are essential for seamless virtual connections.

Potential Earnings

Earnings for online mealtime companions can vary based on factors such as experience, the frequency of sessions, and the demand for their services:

Entry-Level Companions: Those starting out might charge modest fees, often ranging from $10 to $30 per mealtime session.

Experienced Companions: As they build a reputation and loyal clientele, companions can potentially earn in the range of $30 to $100 per session or more.

Specialized Companions: Those who specialize in particular cuisines or offer unique mealtime experiences may command higher rates.

Conclusion

In the age of digital connections, where screens often stand as barriers to human interaction, online mealtime companions serve as heartwarming reminders that technology can also bridge divides and nourish the human spirit. They transform solitary mealtimes into moments of warmth and camaraderie, reminding us that even in the virtual world, the simple act of sharing a meal has the power to create cherished memories and lifelong connections. As we explore unconventional online jobs, this chapter unveils the extraordinary role of online mealtime companions and the meaningful connections they bring to dining tables around the world.

Chapter 9: Virtual Traveling Companion

In the ever-evolving realm of online occupations, a truly extraordinary role emerges—the virtual traveling companion. These intrepid individuals embark on digital journeys, offering personalized travel experiences to those who may not have the opportunity to physically travel or who simply seek to explore new horizons from the comfort of their own homes. Through virtual tours, travel tips, real-time footage, and engaging conversations, they transport travelers to far-flung destinations and foster a deep appreciation for the world's diverse cultures and places.

The Essence of a Virtual Traveling Companion

Alex's journey as a virtual traveling companion is a testament to the transformative power of technology and the human spirit of adventure. When he dons his virtual explorer hat, his mission is to not only guide but also to ignite the spark of curiosity and connection in travelers around the world.

1. Planning the Digital Adventure: Alex begins by meticulously planning each virtual travel experience. He selects destinations that resonate with his clients' interests, whether it's the bustling streets of Tokyo, the serene landscapes of New Zealand, or the historic wonders of Rome. His goal is to create an adventure that feels tailored to the traveler's dreams.

2. Crafting Immersive Virtual Tours: Armed with a virtual camera and an engaging narrative, Alex takes travelers on immersive tours of iconic landmarks and hidden gems. Through high-quality videos and interactive platforms, he provides a 360-degree view of the world's wonders. Whether it's strolling through ancient ruins or savoring the sights and sounds of vibrant markets, Alex's virtual tours transport travelers to distant lands.

3. Sharing Cultural Insights: Alex understands that travel isn't just about seeing new places; it's about understanding the people and cultures that inhabit them. He engages in conversations about local traditions, customs, and cuisines, offering travelers a window into the heart of each destination. Through discussions with locals, language lessons, and live Q&A sessions, he fosters cross-cultural connections.

4. Real-Time Adventures: For the adventurous souls who seek spontaneity, Alex provides real-time adventures. With a stable internet connection and a mobile device, he takes travelers on journeys through bustling streets, vibrant festivals, and breathtaking natural landscapes. Whether it's experiencing a local market's hustle and bustle or witnessing a sunrise over a tranquil beach, these real-time adventures capture the essence of the moment.

5. Personalized Travel Tips: Beyond the virtual experience, Alex equips travelers with personalized travel tips. He shares packing recommendations, suggests off-the-beaten-path experiences, and provides practical advice for navigating different destinations. These tips empower travelers to plan their own adventures in the future.

6. Fostering a Sense of Connection: At the heart of Alex's virtual traveling companionship is the desire to foster connections. He encourages travelers to share their own travel stories, dreams, and aspirations. Through shared experiences and discussions, he creates a community of like-minded explorers who support and inspire each other.

7. Catering to Special Needs: Alex is particularly sensitive to the needs of travelers with physical limitations. He ensures that virtual experiences are accessible and enjoyable for everyone, making the world of travel inclusive.

8. Post-Adventure Reflections: After each virtual journey, Alex encourages travelers to reflect on their experiences. He facilitates discussions where travelers can share their favorite moments, insights gained, and the impact of the adventure on their perspective of the world.

For Alex, being a virtual traveling companion is not just a job; it's a calling driven by a passion for exploration and a deep commitment to making the world accessible to all. Through the lens of his virtual camera and the warmth of his conversations, he opens doors to understanding, empathy, and shared experiences, proving that the spirit of adventure knows no boundaries, whether physical or digital.

The Beauty of Virtual Travel

The allure of virtual traveling companions lies in their ability to create vivid travel experiences:

1. *Virtual Tours: They take travelers on immersive virtual tours of iconic landmarks, historic sites, bustling markets, and picturesque landscapes, allowing them to explore the world's wonders from their screens.*

2. *Travel Tips and Insights: Virtual companions share invaluable travel tips, from packing hacks to cultural dos and don'ts. They provide insights that empower travelers to navigate new territories confidently.*

3. *Real-Time Footage: With the power of live streaming, they offer real-time footage of their own travels, giving travelers a front-row seat to the world's beauty, festivals, and daily life.*

4. *Cultural Exchange: These companions engage in conversations about various cultures, traditions, and cuisines. They facilitate dialogues between travelers and locals, fostering cross-cultural connections.*

The Requirements

Becoming a virtual traveling companion requires a combination of qualities and skills:

Passion for Travel: A deep love for exploration and a curiosity about the world's diverse cultures are at the core of this role.

Communication Skills: The ability to convey the essence of travel through engaging conversations and storytelling is essential.

Tech Proficiency: Proficiency in video conferencing and streaming platforms ensures seamless virtual travel experiences.

Empathy and Patience: Compassion and patience are vital when helping travelers fulfill their travel dreams, especially those who may face physical limitations.

Potential Earnings

Earnings for virtual traveling companions can vary based on factors like experience, specialization, and the demand for their services:

Entry-Level Companions: Beginners may charge around $20 to $50 per virtual travel experience.

Experienced Companions: With growing expertise and a loyal clientele, companions can potentially earn between $50 and $100 or more per virtual travel session.

Specialized Companions: Those who specialize in unique destinations or offer tailored experiences may command higher rates.

Conclusion

In the age of digital connectivity, where the world's boundaries are blurred by the magic of technology, virtual traveling companions serve as ambassadors of exploration and connection. They unlock the world's wonders for all who yearn for adventure, proving that even in the virtual realm, the thrill of discovery, the appreciation of diverse cultures, and the joy of shared experiences know no bounds. As we journey through the realm of unconventional online jobs, this chapter unveils the remarkable role of virtual traveling companions and their ability to make the world accessible to all, one digital journey at a time.

Chapter 10: Online Gym Companionship

In the dynamic landscape of online careers, a role that embodies health, fitness, and inspiration thrives—the online gym companion. These fitness enthusiasts serve as digital motivators, supporting individuals in their fitness journeys through virtual workout sessions, exercise demonstrations, and personalized fitness plans. They offer not only guidance but also encouragement, accountability, and fitness advice, making strides toward healthier and more active lives accessible from the comfort of one's own home.

The Heart of Online Gym Companionship

Meet Sarah, an online gym companion whose passion for fitness is infectious. By day, she works in a corporate office, navigating the intricacies of project management. However, when her virtual gym doors swing open, Sarah transforms into a beacon of motivation and well-being.

Sarah's journey as an online gym companion is a testament to the transformative power of fitness and her unwavering commitment to making health and well-being accessible to all, regardless of their daily schedules or physical locations.

1. Tailoring Personalized Fitness Plans: Sarah starts each fitness journey by getting to know her clients intimately. She learns about their goals, fitness levels, and any unique considerations such as medical conditions or time constraints. With this information, she crafts personalized fitness plans that are both achievable and exciting.

2. Energizing Virtual Workout Sessions: Sarah's virtual gym sessions are the heart of her companionship. Through live video calls, she conducts dynamic workouts that cater to her clients' needs. Whether it's a high-energy HIIT session, a calming yoga practice, or strength training, she ensures that each session is engaging and effective.

3. Guiding with Expertise: As a certified fitness instructor, Sarah places a premium on proper form and technique. During her sessions, she meticulously guides her clients through exercises, demonstrating correct posture and movements to prevent injury. Her expertise shines through, instilling confidence and competence in her clients.

4. Fostering Encouragement and Accountability: Sarah's role extends beyond physical exercise; she provides emotional support and motivation. She checks in with her clients regularly, ensuring they stay accountable to their fitness commitments. She celebrates their victories, no matter how small, and helps them overcome hurdles with a positive mindset.

5. Educating on Holistic Fitness: Recognizing that fitness is only one facet of well-being, Sarah shares insights on nutrition, recovery, and mental health. She educates her clients on the holistic nature of fitness, empowering them to make healthier lifestyle choices.

6. Building a Fitness Community: Sarah fosters a sense of community among her clients. Through group workout sessions and online forums, she creates a supportive network where clients can share their progress, challenges, and successes. This community becomes a source of inspiration and camaraderie.

7. Adaptability and Flexibility: Sarah understands that life is unpredictable, and schedules can be erratic. She offers flexible training times and adapts workout routines to accommodate her clients' changing needs.

8. Celebrating Transformations: One of Sarah's greatest joys is witnessing her clients' transformations. She celebrates their improved fitness levels, increased energy, and enhanced well-being. These success stories serve as testaments to her dedication and the power of her guidance.

Sarah's virtual gym companionship transcends the confines of the digital screen. Through her passion, expertise, and unwavering support, she not only helps her clients achieve their fitness goals but also inspires them to embrace a healthier and more active lifestyle. She is a beacon of motivation and well-being, proving that the path to fitness and vitality can be navigated from the comfort of one's own home, no matter the demands of the daily grind.

The Significance of Fitness Motivation

The allure of online gym companions lies in their ability to create meaningful fitness experiences:

1. *Virtual Workout Sessions: They lead virtual workout sessions, catering to a wide range of fitness levels and goals. From high-intensity interval training (HIIT) to yoga and strength training, they guide clients through workouts that are customized to their needs.*

2. *Exercise Demonstrations: Through live video demonstrations, they teach clients proper exercise techniques, ensuring safety and effectiveness. They demystify fitness equipment and routines, making them accessible to beginners.*

3. *Personalized Fitness Plans: Online gym companions craft personalized fitness plans based on clients' goals, schedules, and fitness levels. These plans serve as roadmaps to healthier lives, tailored to each individual's unique journey.*

4. *Encouragement and Accountability: Beyond physical guidance, they offer emotional support and motivation. They hold clients accountable for their fitness commitments, helping them overcome obstacles and stay on track.*

5. *Fitness Advice and Education: They provide valuable insights on nutrition, recovery, and overall well-being. They educate clients on the importance of holistic fitness, empowering them to make informed choices.*

The Requirements

Becoming an online gym companion necessitates a combination of qualities and skills:

Passion for Fitness: A deep love for fitness and well-being is the driving force behind this role.

Certifications: Many online gym companions hold certifications in personal training, yoga instruction, or group fitness instruction to ensure they provide safe and effective guidance.

Communication Skills: The ability to motivate and engage clients through virtual platforms is crucial.

Empathy and Patience: A compassionate and patient approach is vital when helping clients navigate their fitness journeys.

Potential Earnings

Earnings for online gym companions can vary based on factors such as experience, specialization, and the demand for their services:

Entry-Level Companions: Beginners may charge around $20 to $50 per virtual workout session.

Experienced Companions: With a growing clientele and expertise, companions can potentially earn between $50 and $100 or more per session.

Specialized Companions: Those who specialize in specific fitness niches or offer unique training experiences may command higher rates.

Conclusion

In the digital age, where screens often stand as barriers to physical activity, online gym companions rise as champions of health and fitness. They inspire, guide, and empower individuals to embark on transformative fitness journeys, proving that the path to well-being can be navigated from the convenience of one's own home. As we explore unconventional online careers, this chapter unveils the remarkable role of online gym companions and their potential to transform lives, one virtual workout at a time.

Conclusion

In the ever-evolving landscape of the digital era, the concept of careers has transcended traditional boundaries. The journey we've embarked upon within these pages has been one of discovery, innovation, and possibility. From virtual friendship to online travel companionship, from personal historians to digital confidants, we've explored a realm of unconventional online careers that not only exist but thrive in our interconnected world.

As we conclude this exploration, we stand at the crossroads of innovation and human connection. These unconventional online careers represent the fusion of technology and humanity, where screens become portals to understanding, empathy, and opportunity. Each chapter has unveiled a unique facet of the digital universe, introducing individuals who have harnessed the power of technology to create meaningful connections, share stories, offer support, and redefine the very essence of work.

In our journey, we've met Sarah, who becomes a virtual friend when the world feels lonely; Alex, who takes us on virtual journeys to far-off lands; Robert, who preserves the stories that define us; and countless others who have carved out unconventional paths that illuminate the boundless possibilities of the digital age.

Through these careers, we've witnessed the resilience of the human spirit, the power of empathy, and the profound impact of connection. We've learned that in a world often characterized by screens and distances, it is the warmth of human interaction that remains at the heart of every endeavor.

As we turn the final page, we realize that the digital age offers not only career opportunities but also a canvas for creativity, compassion, and community. Unconventional online careers are not just about making a living; they are about making a difference, one virtual connection at a time.

In the chapters of this book, we've embarked on a journey beyond boundaries, and in doing so, we've uncovered the limitless potential of the human spirit. As we look to the future, let us remember that our screens can be bridges, our digital interactions can be profound, and our unconventional careers can be pathways to a more connected, compassionate, and innovative world.

So, to all the digital pioneers, the virtual companions, the online trailblazers, and the unconventional career enthusiasts, remember this: Your journey has just begun, and the possibilities are as boundless as the digital universe itself. Embrace the future, continue to explore, and never cease to connect, for in the digital age, the world is your canvas, and your impact is immeasurable.